# MINECRAFT:
## Redstone and Transportation

**CHERRY LAKE PUBLISHING • ANN ARBOR, MICHIGAN**

**by James Zeiger**

A Note to Adults: Please review the instructions for the activities in this book before allowing children to do them. Be sure to help them with any activities you do not think they can safely complete on their own.

A Note to Kids: Be sure to ask an adult for help with these activities when you need it. Always put your safety first!

Published in the United States of America by Cherry Lake Publishing
Ann Arbor, Michigan
www.cherrylakepublishing.com

Reading Adviser: Marla Conn, Read With Me Now
Photo Credits: Cover and pages 4, 15, 17–18, and 20, James Zeiger;
page 5, Ares C.; pages 7–8, 11–13, 25, and 27, Sebastian Olsen;
pages 22, 29, Piper Keltner.

Library of Congress Cataloging-in-Publication Data
Library of Congress Cataloging-in-Publication data on file.

Cherry Lake Publishing would like to acknowledge the work of The Partnership for
21st Century Skills. Please visit *www.p21.org* for more information.

Printed in the United States of America
Corporate Graphics
January 2016

# Contents

Chapter 1

# Bringing Creations to Life

You've created huge buildings and mined rare gems. You've walked through forests, deserts, and grasslands. You've scaled mountains and swum through the ocean. Your wheat, potatoes, and other crops are thriving. Your livestock are healthy and growing in number. What more could you ask for in your *Minecraft* life? Plenty!

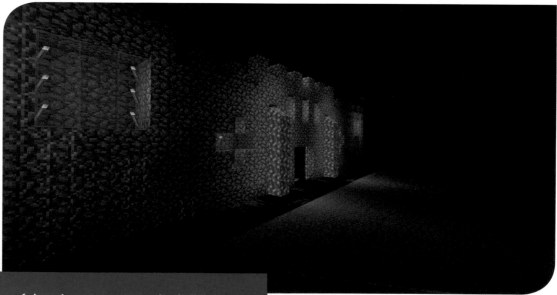

*Minecraft* doesn't stop at constructing buildings.

Imagine there is a substance that can power the world around you. You can lay it down like electrical wiring on any solid block. Or you can add it to objects to make them light up, move, or explode. This substance even brings a little bit of magic when mixed with just the right ingredients. What is this wonderful material? Redstone!

Nothing quite like redstone exists in the real world. In some ways, redstone works a lot like electricity does. Both provide energy. But unlike electricity, redstone is a solid material. Each piece of redstone produces a

## Unlimited Possibilities

Once you have redstone, you can use it to build countless different creations. You can power a cart or a sliding glass door. You could build a sidewalk that lights up at night or a room where the lights turn on when you walk in. Hook it up to a block of TNT and cause an explosion! Or you can think even bigger. One person constructed a working calculator! What marvelous machines will you create?

signal. At its full power of 15, the signal travels as far as 15 blocks to power a machine or light a lamp. However, the signal fades a bit with each block.

You can obtain redstone in a number of ways. The most straightforward method is to mine it. It is most often found deep underground, where the rarest pieces of **ore** are more common. You can recognize redstone ore by the flecks of red in the otherwise gray block. To mine it, it's best to use an iron pickaxe or, even better, a diamond one. One block of redstone ore produces four or five redstone dusts (often simply called redstones). You can also **smelt** redstone ore by burning it in a furnace. Any fuel works for this, from coal or wood to lava.

Redstone also naturally appears in a few places. Destroy a trap in any jungle temple and you'll be able to gather the redstone that was powering it. This can yield as many as 15 redstones. If you find a chest in a

Dungeon chests sometimes contain redstone.

dungeon, in a stronghold altar or storeroom, or in an abandoned mine, look inside. There's a small chance you'll find redstone there. You have the highest chance—just over 50 percent—of finding redstone in a dungeon chest. However, you'll only find between one and four redstones at a time. In other chests, the chances of finding redstones are much lower, but you could find as many as nine redstones at once. You can also trade an emerald for redstone with a cleric in a village. Another option is to gather it from witches. Whenever a witch dies, she drops between zero and six redstones.

**Chapter 2**

# Redstone Basics

Redstone is a remarkably flexible substance. One way to use its power is to add it to devices as an ingredient. Combine it with four iron **ingots** to make a compass. Add redstone to four gold ingots and you'll craft a clock. A redstone lamp is made up of redstone and glowstone, a special substance that gives off light.

A redstone torch can attach to a wall or other object.

A tick is a measurement of time in *Minecraft*. For redstone devices, one tick is equal to 0.1 seconds. Two ticks is 0.2 seconds, three is 0.3 seconds, and so on.

Redstone can't do much on its own. It needs a few additional parts and pieces for it to reach its potential. One way to use redstone is as a torch. To craft a torch, combine a stick with one redstone. A redstone torch isn't like a regular *Minecraft* torch. Redstone torches give out much less light. As a result, they can't help crops grow overnight or keep mobs from spawning in dark places. What a redstone torch *does* do is provide power to itself and the block just above it. Any wiring attached to it is also powered.

You cannot turn a redstone torch on or off by hand. No matter how many times you click on the torch, it'll stay on. However, there is a way to get around this. Redstone torches are inverters. This means they are always on until another redstone signal hits them. Then the torch inverts that signal, or does the opposite of what the signal demands. The signal is on, but the torch turns off. There is always a delay (one redstone tick, or 0.1 second) before a redstone torch switches on or off. Keep this in mind when you build **circuits**.

Another way to use redstone is as wiring. Lay the wire down on any solid block with the Use action. However, redstone wiring is useless without a power source. A redstone torch or a block of redstone would both work. A redstone block is fairly straightforward to make—just combine nine redstones.

Remember that you cannot turn these power sources on or off directly. However, there are other power sources to use. You can turn a lever, button, or pressure plate on or off by hand. Each of these power sources works slightly differently and best fits different situations. A lever is a lot like the switch you use to turn the lights on when you enter a room. Move the lever to the up position with the Use action, and the power is on. Move the lever down, and the power turns off. A button releases a single, short pulse of power

## Quick Tip: Switching Off the Torch

You cannot click on a redstone torch to turn it off. But you can turn it off by clicking something else: a lever, button, or pressure plate. Attach any of these power sources to a redstone torch or to the same block the torch is attached to. Activate the lever, button, or pressure plate, and the torch turns off. The reverse is true, too. To turn the torch back on, just turn the other power source off.

On the block on the left, the lever is off and the redstone torch is on. On the right, the lever is on and the torch is off.

when you push it. Attach either of these devices to a solid block, and they power both themselves and the block they're attached to. If you have a pressure plate, put it on top of a solid block. Standing on the plate turns the power on. Step off the pressure plate, and the power switches off. A pressure plate powers itself and the block just below it.

Redstone wire has to have one end attached directly to its power source. Beyond that, it can travel up, down, or sideways as long as it's on a solid block. There are some limitations, though. **Transparent** blocks such as glass or specially crafted objects such

## Repeater Delays

A repeater automatically adds a delay of one redstone tick. However, you can add a longer delay. Maybe you're trying to perfectly time a trap for enemies. Or perhaps you need your automatic doors to open at just the right moment. Just click the repeater once with the Use action to increase the delay to two ticks, or 0.2 seconds. One of the two prongs on top of the device moves one notch away from the other prong. Click it again for three ticks, and the prong moves again. Four ticks is the most you'll get. If you click the repeater again, it will circle back to one tick.

as stairs can't carry the **current**. Also, the wire can only go up or down one block at a time. If a climb or fall is longer than that, the circuit won't work. So if a wire needs to go higher or lower, it is best to use a step or spiral pattern.

A line of redstone gradually fades to reddish brown as the signal fades.

A redstone repeater allows a redstone signal to travel longer than 15 blocks.

Redstone's signal is limited. At its most powerful, it reaches 15 blocks. But what if you have a circuit that requires a longer distance between the power source and an object? You can extend a power source's reach with a special device called a repeater. A repeater "repeats" a signal, boosting it back up to 15. Use as many repeaters as you need to complete a circuit and make it work. Remember: Power only travels one direction through a repeater. Make sure you set up your circuit so the current travels the correct direction through the repeater. Otherwise, it won't work.

**Chapter 3**

# Useful Structures

**W**hat can you do with redstone? The answer is just about anything. With a bit of experimentation and some trial and error, you'll pick up a lot of tricks as you go. You'll also see firsthand that there are often countless different ways to do the same thing. The only limit is your creativity. If you're just starting out, you might want to start small.

Have you ever visited a store where the doors opened automatically when you stood in front of

Many larger stores have automatic sliding doors.

them? You didn't even have to touch them. In *Minecraft*, an automatic door is one of the easier circuits to build, so let's try it.

For the whole project, you'll need:

- 7 blocks of any solid material for building
- 2 redstone torches
- 4 sticky pistons
- 30–40 redstone
- 4 pressure plates

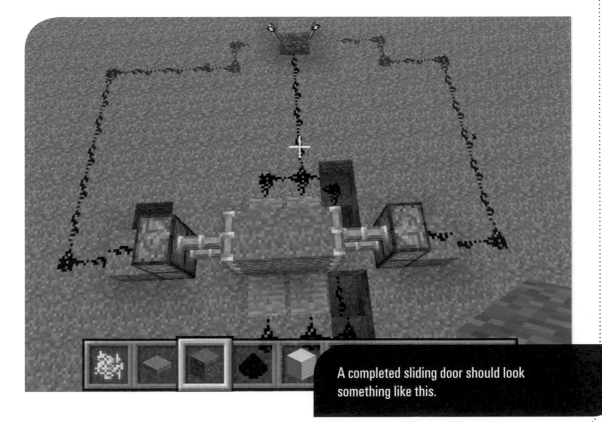

A completed sliding door should look something like this.

First, we'll build a **generator**. This will provide a main source of power for the automatic door. Place one building block on the ground five or six spaces from where you plan to build your door. Attach two redstone torches to opposite sides of the block.

Next, place the sticky pistons. These will make up the outer sides of the door. Put them in two stacks. Each one should be two pistons tall. The stacks should have four empty spaces between them, with the pistons facing each another.

Place one building block on the ground behind each bottom piston. Starting at the top of each block, lay a line of redstone dust down the back of the block on the farthest side from the piston. Make sure the line points at the piston. Connect the other end to each of

## Working with Real-World Circuits

Circuits are a huge part of day-to-day life in the real world. They turn on your lights, power your television, and even make it possible to play *Minecraft*. The people in charge of creating, updating, and maintaining these circuits are electricians and electrical engineers. Unlike redstone, electricity can be extremely dangerous. It takes years of training to safely and successfully add wiring to a home, business, street, or any other location. So next time you flip a switch or power up your laptop, remember there's someone to thank for the spark that runs it!

Run redstone wire from the pistons on each side to the generator.

the torches on the generator. If everything is correct, all four pistons should be extended. The redstone will also be powered. You'll know the wire is powered if it's bright red. Unpowered redstone is a duller, red-brown color.

Now you can add in the actual door. Fill in the space between the extended pistons with the remaining building blocks. Stack them two blocks wide and two blocks high. In front of each side of the door, lay the pressure plates in twos on the ground.

Next, we need to connect the pressure plates in a circuit. Start by placing redstone dust in the square in

Connect the pressure plates to each other by digging a tunnel under the pistons.

front of each pressure plate. Then mine a tunnel under each stack of pistons. If you dig deeper than one level down, remember to include steps leading down in the tunnel. Once it is done, lay redstone through the tunnel and connect it to the pressure plates. Finally, connect that circuit directly to a side of the generator that hasn't been used yet.

Now you can use the door! Stand on the pressure plates, and the door will open. When you're not standing on a plate, the door will stay closed.

Why does it work? The generator keeps the pistons extended. This keeps your door closed. When you stand on the pressure plates, you turn them on. Their power hits the redstone torches on the generator and turns them off. The pistons collapse, and the doors open. This takes advantage of the fact that a redstone torch is an inverter.

Another concept that forms a basis for redstone creations is delays. To start experimenting with these, we can use repeaters. For this project, you'll need:

- 5 dirt blocks
- 5 redstone torches
- 1 lever
- 15–20 redstone
- 5 redstone repeaters

To start, place the five dirt blocks in a row on the ground, with one empty space between each. Place a redstone torch on top of each block. Then put the lever a few spaces away from the line. On the ground in front of each dirt block, lay a line of redstone two spaces long. The lines should all go in the same direction, **perpendicular** to the line of blocks.

Next, add a redstone repeater at the end of each line of redstone extending from the dirt blocks. Pay attention to the direction the repeaters face. Every time you place one, it will automatically face where you're standing. So when you place a repeater, make sure you're looking in the direction you want the current to travel. For this project, you'll want to face the lever.

Once they're placed, face each repeater and tap the Use button to adjust the repeater's delay. Set all of

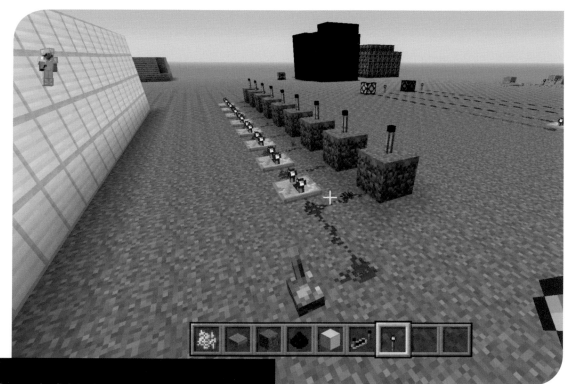

When you're finished, your repeater circuit will look similar to this.

them to the maximum possible: four ticks. When the repeater is at this setting, the movable prong on top will be as far from the other prong as possible.

Right now, all the torches should be lit, and the repeaters should be off. Connect the line of repeaters to the lever with redstone. Now, switch the lever on with the Use action. The redstone current should travel through each repeater with a visible delay. Watch as each torch turns off one by one.

These are just a couple of ways to play with redstone. You can apply these same concepts to a range of other creations. Add more circuits, multiple generators, or more complicated combinations of torches, repeaters, and switches. See what you can do!

Chapter 4

# Redstone on the Rails

**W**alking can take you just about anywhere in *Minecraft*. However, it can take quite a while to reach someplace outside of your immediate area. Moving cargo such as animals, food, or ore takes even longer. Luckily, there's a solution. Rails to the rescue!

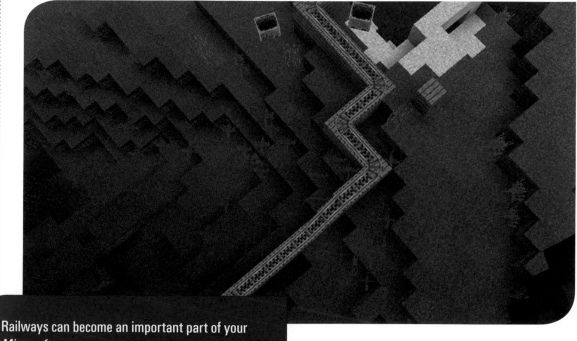

Railways can become an important part of your *Minecraft* game.

**Quick Tip: Need a Break?**

A mine cart will naturally lose **momentum** if it travels up a slope or along a long stretch of regular track. You can slow it down faster, though, by hitting the "Backward" movement button. If you want to be fancy—or if you won't be in the car—use powered rails. A powered rail needs to be connected to a redstone power source in order to be activated. If the rail isn't activated, it slows down any cart that passes over it. Two nonactivated power rails are enough to stop a mine cart in most situations. But if a cart is traveling down a slope at top speed, you might need three rails to come to a complete stop.

Rails in *Minecraft* allow you to create tracks for mine carts. These carts can carry just about anything, including you! You have probably run into carts and rails if you've explored any abandoned mines. If you attack and destroy a cart with a weapon, you can pick it up. You can mine rails with a pickaxe.

A more reliable method is just to build your own. To craft a mine cart, you need five iron ingots. Three go in a line along the bottom row of squares on your crafting table. One goes in the middle square on the left, and one goes in the middle square on the right. Combine a mine cart with certain ingredients on your crafting table to give your cart special abilities. TNT, a chest, or a furnace on a mine cart all make these useful objects mobile.

All you need for a standard rail is a stick and six iron ingots. In your crafting grid, put the stick in the center square. Place three iron ingots in a row down the left side and three on the right side of the grid. Standard rails are a necessity. They're the only rail you can use to create turns in the track.

There are three types of special rail, and they power your cart along the track. This is where redstone comes in. A powered rail is the one you'll likely use the most. When you connect one of these rails to a redstone power source, the rail launches a mine cart forward. You can use them to start a cart on its journey or to give it extra speed along the way. To make a powered rail, swap out the iron ingots for gold

## Quick Tip: Two-Way Traffic

A detector rail/powered rail setup only works if the powered rail is positioned after the detector rail. If you only ever travel one direction on your track, this isn't a problem. But what if you want to travel both directions? Add another detector rail on the opposite side of the powered rail. This way, the cart will hit a detector rail, then a powered rail, no matter which way it's traveling.

Powered rails need a power source, such as a redstone torch.

ones when crafting. Add redstone dust to the bottom center square.

A detector rail is made with iron ingots and redstone dust. A pressure plate replaces the usual stick in the crafting grid. When a cart passes over one of these rails, the rail sends out a redstone signal. The signal can be used just as any other redstone signal. Maybe

**Quick Tip: Going Up?**

Without powered rails or a character to push it, the cart can only travel up a slope for a few blocks. To keep it going, add a powered rail every other block or so.

it sets off an explosion, causes a switch in the track ahead, or just opens a door. Detector rails can also be used as power sources for any powered rail directly attached to it. As the cart passes over the detector rail, it activates the powered rail ahead. This gives the cart a boost of speed.

The third special rail is called an activator rail. It triggers activity in the cart itself. If the cart carries TNT, the TNT will explode. If you or any mob are inside, you'll be thrown out.

You can place rails on any solid block. Create slopes by building solid blocks up in a step pattern, moving up one level at a time. To add turns, use a standard rail. You'll need to provide power for your cart to move. You can do this using the Forward button if you're on board. But you'll need powered rails if you're not on board. Powered rails need to be connected to a power source. Just like any other redstone device, this can be a lever, button, pressure plate, redstone torch, or redstone block. It can also be a detector rail. When one powered rail is active, the signal travels as far as nine blocks. Beyond that, you will need another power source. The source can be located in any block immediately touching the rail— even below it.

There are a lot of complicated things you can do with a *Minecraft* rail system. Four-way intersections,

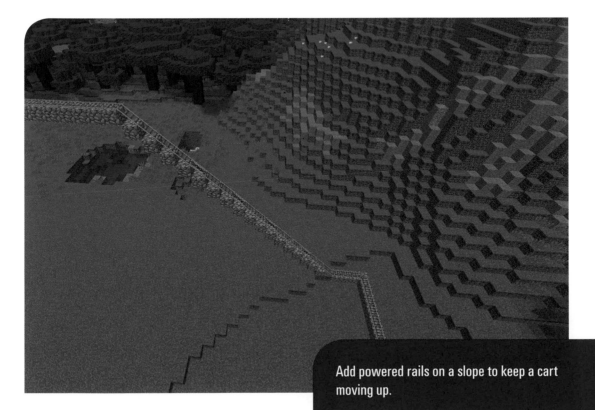

Add powered rails on a slope to keep a cart moving up.

switching points, and other structures are all possibilities. However, since we're just starting out, let's start with the most important part of the railway: the starting point.

A starting point is pretty easy to set up. If you'll be riding in the cart, you can just place a block of any solid material at the end of the track. Plop a cart in front of the block, and hit the Use button to climb in. Look forward down the track, and hit the Forward button. Your cart will move forward.

If you don't want to keep your finger on the Forward button the whole time, add power. You'll need a block of any solid material, a power source (a button or lever works well), and one powered rail. Lay your powered rail at the end of your tracks. Next, place your block of solid material just after the powered rail, where there are no tracks. Attach the button

## Real World Rails

Railroads aren't just a way to get around *Minecraft*. They're also a huge part of transportation in the real world. They carry passengers, packages, and countless other types of cargo. Specially designed high-speed passenger trains can travel as fast as 374 miles (602 kilometers) per hour! These trains rely on magnets to move that fast, and they require special tracks to reach top speeds.

Your rail system may become very complex!

or lever to the top of the block that faces the tracks. When you're ready to go, set a cart on the powered rails and switch the power on. Remember that a button provides a pulse of power. Use that if you want the power to immediately turn off on its own. Use a lever if you want the power to stay on until you switch it off.

Once you are started, where you go is up to you. Do you want to build a roller coaster? Transport crops or cattle? Travel between your many grand homes? Your options are unlimited!

# Glossary

**circuits** (SIR-kits) complete paths for electrical current to follow

**current** (CUR-uhnt) the movement of electricity

**generator** (JEN-uh-ray-tur) a machine that produces power

**ingots** (ING-guhts) masses of metal that have been shaped into bars

**momentum** (moh-MEN-tuhm) the speed something gains as it moves

**ore** (OR) rock or soil that contains metal or valuable minerals

**perpendicular** (pur-pen-DIK-yoo-lur) a line that is at right angles to another line or to a surface

**smelt** (SMELT) to melt ore so the metal can be removed

**transparent** (trans-PARE-uhnt) clear like glass; transparent material lets light through so objects on the other side can be seen

# Find Out More

## BOOKS

Farwell, Nick. *Minecraft: Redstone Handbook*. New York: Scholastic, 2014.

Miller, Megan. *The Ultimate Unofficial Encyclopedia for Minecrafters: An A–Z of Tips and Tricks the Official Guides Don't Teach You*. New York: Skyhorse Publishing, Inc., 2015.

Monk, Matthew. *Minecraft Mastery: Build Your Own Redstone Contraptions and Mods*. New York: McGraw-Hill Education, 2014.

## WEB SITES

### For Dummies: Engineering with Redstone in Minecraft

*www.dummies.com/how-to/content/engineering-with-redstone-in-minecraft.html*

Find out more about how redstone works.

### Minecraft101—Redstone 101

*www.minecraft101.net/redstone/redstone101.html*

This site offers links to basic information on redstone and rails. There are also some how-tos for basic redstone creations.

# Index

## About the Author

James Zeiger is a student at the Missouri University of Science and Technology. An avid gamer, his lifelong interest in engineering naturally led him to Minecraft.